W9-BYB-563

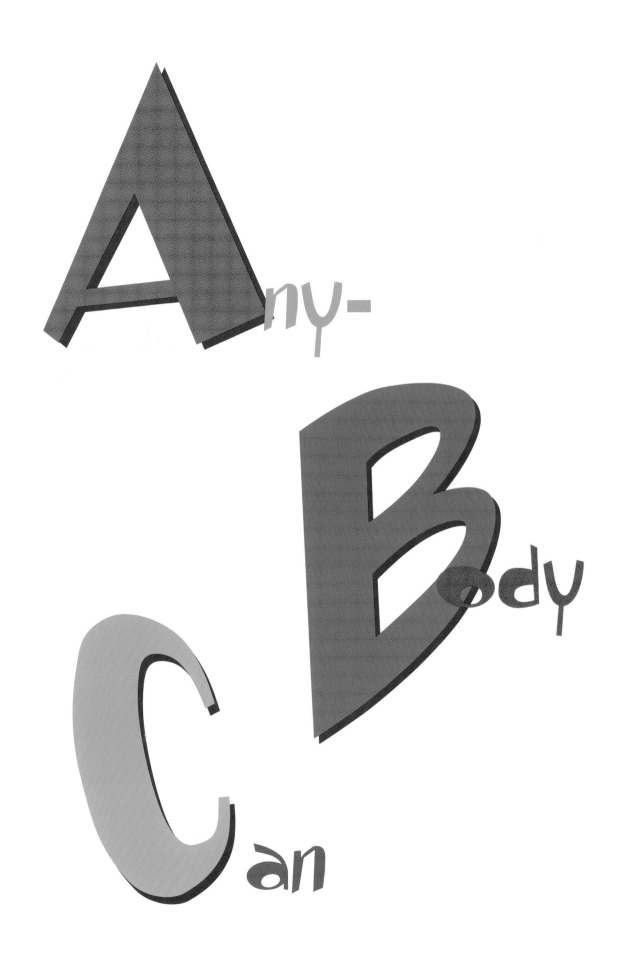

To My Family
To You and Yours
To Motivationeers Whom Inspire and Motivate Us
To Teachers — Heroes at Work

"You can become the person you want to be."
— Dr. Robert H. Schuller

Any- **B**ody **C**an

Parents Choice Press
U.S.A.

Anybody, anybody,
Anybody can
Believe it, achieve it
Plan, plan, plan
Anybody, anybody,
Anybody can.

B

b

B is for better
B is for best
Always make your good
Better
And make your better
Best.

**C is for choice
Decisions, decisions
The power to choose
The greatest power
on earth
Just for me to use.**

D
d

A dream is a desire
A want, a need,
Be determined
Don't quit
You will succeed.

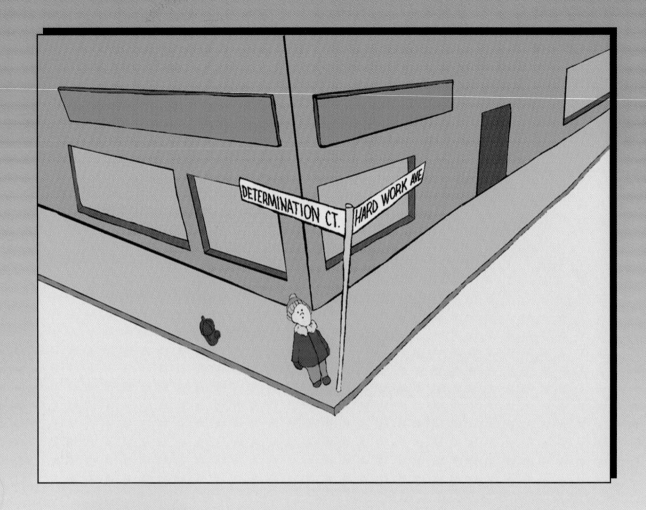

**Easy Street Easy Street
Much to my regret
I still haven't found
An Easy Street yet
But, the harder I work
The easier it gets.**

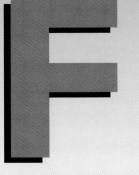

**F is for faith
The rules we trust
Guidelines for me
Because I'm loved
So much.**

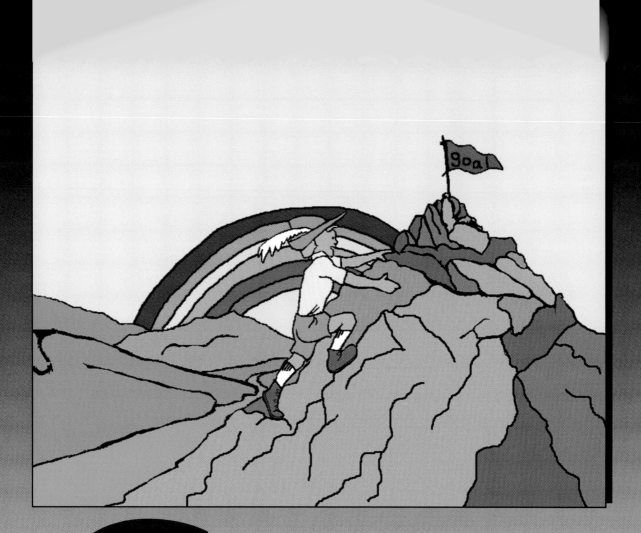

G
g

G is for goal
The rainbow's end
There isn't a kit for
Which you can send
So get up, get up
And go for it,
My friend.

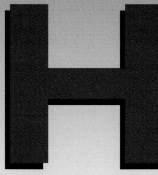

Hope is courage,
Thank you — please
We're out to uncover
The possibilities.

I i

**When I grow up,
It's my intent
To be, to be intelligent
And then I'll know
That in a pinch
Inch by inch
Anything's a cinch.**

J j

J is for journey
From A–Z
Tell me, tell me
Who do you see?
Why it's ICAN,
ICAN Bee.

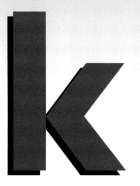

**Knowledge is power
The power of knowing
Listen and learn
And you'll keep on
Growing.**

Love is a gift
To give—to share
It's a special feeling
It shows that you care.

M

m

**Look in the mirror
And see what you see
Anyway you look at it
There's only one me
Me only once
Only one me I see
It must be the best of
Me I see.**

N
n

Now is positively
The best time ever
Me a quitter?
Never, ever.
There is nothing
I can't do
If I decide to
See it through.

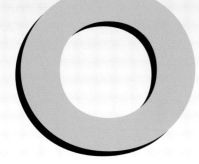

**Opportunity is time
The time is right
Anytime is
Opportunity time
Day or night.**

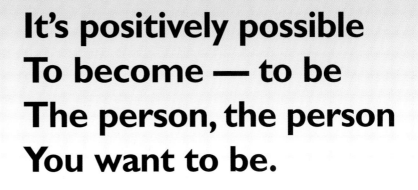

It's positively possible
To become — to be
The person, the person
You want to be.

Q q

The quality of me
My personal essence is
Directly related
To my commitment
To excellence.

**R is for risk
The chance I will take
Dare to be great
It's no mistake.**

S is for sharing
From me to you
It's just like caring
It's what good
Friends do.

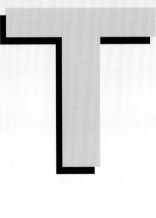

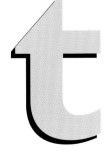

I'm **THINK**
I'm **THANK**
We'd like to say Hi
Our message is simple
Try–try–try.

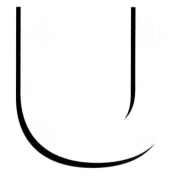

UCAN the toucan
Has something to state
"If others can, you can,
It's never too late".

V is for values
My principles you see
Keystones of character
They're important to me.

W is for will
The will to win
If you want to win,
You must begin.

EXtra! EXtra!
Read all about it
You have ability
Never doubt it.

No matter, no matter
Whatever you do
Always remember
It's up to you.

**Z is for zip
The fuel for winning
Every end is
A new beginning.**

About the Author

Patrick J. Kilbane is a dedicated husband, a father of six outstanding children and a "Motivationeer." Patrick created the AnyBody Can Philosophy using the alphabet to plant the seeds of positive mental attitude not only in his children but every child; he calls this educational and entertaining technique "Motivationeering." Patrick is the managing director of IN-OVO Consulting a management consulting firm specializing in lean manufacturing and continuous improvement. He teaches courses in project management and quality, management and productivity for the University of Phoenix. Early in his career he was an automotive industry executive. Born in Cleveland, Ohio Patrick holds a B.S. from the University of Dayton and an M.B.A. from Baldwin-Wallace College. He is a member of the National Speakers Association-Michigan providing customized programs and consulting. Patrick and his family reside in Saline, Michigan.

Copyright 2002 Parents Choice Press

All rights reserved. No part of this work may be reproduced, stored in a retrieval system, transcribed in any form or by any means, including, but not limited to electronic, mechanical, photocopying, recording or other means, without prior written permission.

ISBN 0-9717570-0-3

Printed in the United States of America

10 9 8 7 6 5 4 3 2 1

For further information, contact:

Parents Choice Press
7461 Steeplechase Drive
Saline, MI 48176

Phone: 734-944-3328
Or visit our website:
www.parentschoicepress.com

Child Development

ABC AnyBody Can, an inspirational and educational book for all adults who live and work with young children, uses the alphabet, rhyme and pictures to impact child development in a positive manner. We call our educational and entertaining technique "motivationeering."

My promise to you is that your child will have a better attitude and you will notice it. Your child will benefit from being exposed to the following concepts: Achievement, dreams, beliefs, faith, hope, love self-esteem, and values. You want your child to be exposed to these concepts in order to better handle life's challenges.

"The simple wisdom of ABC Any Body Can is, as profoundly useful as the alphabet upon which this book is based."
> – Nick Synko, Author Future@Work
> *An Employee Survival Guide for the 21st Century.*

Pat didn't discover what positive mental attitude (PMA) was until he was in his thirties. After he did, his career took off like a rocket. He knew he had to instill this in his children at an early age so that it would become part of their personality and give them an advantage in life. The "proof is in the pudding." Today Pat and his wife Marianne have six outstanding well balanced children, living testimony that his "AnyBody Can" philosophy works. Now you can share his motivationeering technique with your loved ones.

Thank you for considering this book. Make the right choice — be a motivationeer — buy the book and use this opportunity to create value in the life of a child. Plant these seeds and watch them grow. Please tell someone you know about ABC AnyBody Can, they will be glad you did and so will you.

www.abcanybodycan.com